STARTING OUT

baby GUINEA PIGS

LAURA K. MURRAY

CREATIVE EDUCATION • CREATIVE PAPERBACKS

CONT

ENTS

I AM A PUP.

I am a baby guinea pig.

Look at my whiskers and soft fur!

I was born with fur and teeth.
I weighed only 3.5 ounces (100 grams).

I could run! I could eat solid food. My mother fed me milk.

Now I eat hay made from grass. Pellets are part of my meals. I munch on vegetables and fruits, too.

Chewing is good for my teeth!

My house is safe and dark. I can hide or sleep there.

Tunnels and ramps make great places to run. I jump around when I am excited. This little move is called popcorning!

SPEAK AND LISTEN

UT! CHUT! CHUT!

Can you speak like a pup? Guinea pigs make a lot of sounds! They squeak, click, whistle, and purr.

Listen to these sounds:

Now it is your turn!

GUINEA PIG WORDS

hay: plants like grass that have been cut and dried to feed animals

pellet: a small, hard piece of food for pets

popcorning: doing small jumps or spins, often to show excitement

whisker: a thin, stiff hair on an animal's face

READING CORNER

Hansen, Grace. *Guinea Pigs in the Wild!* Minneapolis: Pop!, 2024.

Leaf, Christina. *Guinea Pigs.* Minneapolis: Bellwether Media, 2021.

Rossiter, Brienna. *My Pet Guinea Pig.* Mendota Heights, Minn.: Little Blue House, 2022.

INDEX

PUBLISHED BY CREATIVE EDUCATION AND CREATIVE PAPERBACKS
P.O. Box 227, Mankato, Minnesota 56002
Creative Education and Creative Paperbacks are imprints of The Creative Company
www.thecreativecompany.us

LIBRARY OF CONGRESS CATALOGING-IN-PUBLICATION DATA
Names: Murray, Laura K., 1989- author
Title: Baby guinea pigs / Laura K. Murray.
Description: Mankato, Minnesota : Creative Education and Creative Paperbacks, [2026] | Series: Starting out | Includes bibliographical references and index. | Audience: Ages 4-7 | Audience: Grades K-1 | Summary: "Introduce beginning readers to the world of baby guinea pigs with this life science starter. Includes photos, a labeled animal diagram, "Speak and Listen" section, glossary, and further resources—Provided by publisher.
Identifiers: LCCN 2025015276 (print) | LCCN 2025015277 (ebook) | ISBN 9798895810323 library binding | ISBN 9781682779859 paperback | ISBN 9798895811580 ebook
Subjects: LCSH: Guinea pigs—Infancy—Juvenile literature | Guinea pigs—Juvenile literature
Classification: LCC SF401.G85 M87 2026 (print) | LCC SF401.G85 (ebook) |
DDC 599.35/921392--dc23/eng/20250610
LC record available at https://lccn.loc.gov/2025015276
LC ebook record available at https://lccn.loc.gov/2025015277

DESIGN AND PRODUCTION
Design by Rhea Magaro
Art direction by Graham Morgan

PHOTOGRAPHS BY
Dreamstime/Anettphoto, 2, Azaliya, 10, Chernetskaya, 12, Chrispethick, 4, Diman Oshchepkov, 7, Igor Dutina, 8, Sierpniowka, 11; Getty Images/Iuliana Niculaie / 500px, 9, Oleksandr Shchus, 6; Shutterstock/Rita_Kochmarjova, cover; Unsplash/Jaroslaw Slodkiewicz, 14, Scott Precious, 5

Printed in the United States